Buttermilk Pancakes with Blueberry Sauce

½ cup plus 2 teaspoons sugar

1 cup flour

1 teaspoon baking powder

½ teaspoon baking soda

1 egg, beaten

¾ cup buttermilk

4 tablespoons butter, melted

2 tablespoons red currant jelly

2 tablespoons apple juice

1 cup fresh or frozen blueberries

For pancakes, in a bowl combine 2 teaspoons sugar and other dry ingredients. Form a well in the center and add egg, buttermilk, and half the melted butter. Beat until smooth. Lightly oil a griddle or heavy cast-iron frying pan and heat over medium flame until hot. Spoon 2 to 3 tablespoons of batter onto hot griddle and cook 2 to 3 minutes, or until bottom side is just brown. Flip pancakes over and cook 30 seconds, or until cooked through. Makes 8 to 10.

For blueberry sauce, combine the remaining butter, remaining sugar, and red currant jelly in a medium saucepan. Bring to a boil over medium heat. Stir in apple juice and blueberries and cook until mixture is slightly thickened and blueberries begin to burst. Makes about 1 cup.

From *Old Fashioned Country Favorites*
Published by Doubleday

Cream Biscuits

1 cup flour	3 tablespoons sweet
1 teaspoon baking powder	butter
¼ teaspoon salt	½ cup heavy cream

Preheat oven to 475°. In a bowl combine dry ingredients. Cut in butter until mixture resembles cornmeal. Stir in cream until a dough forms. Roll out dough on a floured surface to ½″ thickness. Cut out 12 rounds with a 1½″ biscuit cutter. On a baking sheet lined with parchment paper or lightly buttered, bake rounds 8 to 10 minutes, or until golden. Serve with raspberry preserves or assorted jams, jellies, and conserves.
Makes 12.

From *Old Fashioned Country Favorites*
Published by Doubleday

Peach Jam

5 pounds ripe peaches　　5 cups sugar
3 tablespoons lemon juice

Blanch peaches 30 seconds to 1 minute or until skin just breaks. Cool under cold water and peel and pit. Roughly chop peaches and place in a large pot. Add lemon juice and sugar. Allow to sit one hour, then bring to a boil over medium heat. Reduce to low heat and cook, stirring, 1½ to 2 hours, or until mixture thickens. Remove from heat, skim away foam, and quickly transfer into 8 hot, sterilized half-pint jars, leaving ¼″ headspace. Screw on sterilized lids. Process in boiling water bath 15 minutes. Refrigerate after opening.
Makes 8 cups.

From *Old Fashioned Country Favorites*
Published by Doubleday

Individual Chicken Potpies

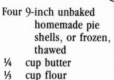

Four 9-inch unbaked homemade pie shells, or frozen, thawed
¼ cup butter
⅓ cup flour
¾ cup milk
1 cup chicken broth
3 cups diced cooked chicken

1 cup diced cooked carrots
1 cup frozen peas, thawed
½ cup frozen pearl onions, thawed
3 tablespoons chopped dill
¼ teaspoon pepper
1 egg, beaten

Preheat oven to 425°. Place piecrusts on a lightly floured board. Cut into four 6½" rounds and fit into 4" pie pans or casseroles. If using frozen crusts, remove from pan and cut to size. Reserve leftover dough. In a medium saucepan, heat butter until melted. Stir in flour until no longer visible. Gradually add milk and broth, stirring until smooth and slightly thick. Add chicken, vegetables, and seasonings, and cook, stirring, until just thickened. Remove from heat. Divide filling among shells. Cut reserved dough into ¼" x 4½" long strips and crisscross into lattice tops. Lightly brush with egg. Place in oven and bake 25 to 30 minutes, or until golden brown. Makes 4.

From *Old Fashioned Country Favorites*
Published by Doubleday

Country Fried Chicken

One 3-pound chicken, cut up
½ cup flour
1 teaspoon salt
¼ teaspoon pepper
Vegetable oil

Rinse chicken and drain thoroughly, but do not pat dry. In a shallow bowl combine flour, salt, and pepper. Press chicken, a piece at a time, in the flour, so that skin is thoroughly coated. In a kettle or deep-fryer add oil to a depth of 1½". Heat over medium-high flame until oil reaches 375°. Gently place chicken into hot oil and fry about 10 minutes per side, or until golden and cooked through. Remove with a slotted spoon onto a plate lined with paper towels. Serve with black-eyed peas, salt pork, corn bread, and buttered mashed potatoes.
Serves 4.

From *Old Fashioned Country Favorites*
Published by Doubleday

Fried Green Tomatoes

4 medium green tomatoes, sliced a scant ½″ thick	½ teaspoon salt
1 egg, lightly beaten	¼ teaspoon pepper
½ cup yellow cornmeal	3 to 4 tablespoons bacon drippings

Dip tomato slices lightly in beaten egg. In a shallow bowl combine dry ingredients. Lightly coat tomato slices on both sides with mixture. In a large skillet heat bacon drippings over medium-high heat until hot but not smoking. Add tomatoes, and fry 2 to 3 minutes, or until lightly browned. Turn tomatoes over and fry until just golden. Shown with thyme sprigs.
Serves 4.

From *Old Fashioned Country Favorites*
Published by Doubleday

Honey-Wheat Bread

1¾ cups milk
⅓ cup vegetable oil
¼ cup honey
2 eggs, beaten
2 cups flour
1½ cups whole wheat flour

⅓ cup wheat flakes, plus
   2 tablespoons for
   sprinkling
1 tablespoon baking
   powder
1 teaspoon baking soda
1 teaspoon salt

Preheat oven to 375°. In a small bowl combine wet ingredients until well combined. In a large bowl combine dry ingredients. Make a well in center and pour in wet ingredients. Stir until just combined and flour is no longer visible. Turn batter into a lightly buttered 9¼" x 5¼" x 2" loaf pan. Soundly rap pan on counter to remove any air pockets. Sprinkle top with remaining wheat flakes. Bake 50 to 55 minutes, or until bread is golden and a toothpick inserted in center comes out clean. Remove from oven and cool 10 minutes. Then turn out onto rack and cool thoroughly before slicing.
Makes 1 loaf.

From *Old Fashioned Country Favorites*
Published by Doubleday

Maple-Glazed Pork Chops

½	teaspoon vegetable oil	3	tablespoons maple syrup
Four	¾″-thick center-cut pork chops		Fresh thyme sprigs
		⅓	cup apple juice

Preheat oven to 325°. In a large cast-iron skillet heat oil over medium-high heat until hot but not smoking. Add pork chops and brown 2 to 3 minutes per side, or until golden. Pour off excess fat. Remove pan from heat, drizzle maple syrup over chops, and place a few thyme sprigs on each one. Add apple juice, cover, and place in oven 45 minutes to 1 hour, or until chops are glazed on bottom and tender. Turn over chops before serving with fresh thyme, buttered biscuits, lima beans, and baked baby pumpkins with cornbread stuffing.
Serves 4.

From *Old Fashioned Country Favorites*
Published by Doubleday

Louisiana Shrimp Boil

6 cups water
2 lemons, halved
2 medium onions, unpeeled
3 tablespoons cider vinegar
1 teaspoon allspice
⅓ cup salt
2 tablespoons yellow mustard seeds
1 tablespoon cayenne pepper

1 teaspoon whole peppercorns
1 teaspoon fennel seeds
1 teaspoon coriander seeds
10 dried red peppers
6 sprigs fresh thyme
4 cloves garlic, peeled
2 bay leaves
2 pounds large shrimp, preferably with heads

In a large nonaluminum pot, bring water to a boil over high heat. Add lemons, onions, and vinegar. Place spices and seasonings in cheesecloth and tie with string. Add to the boiling water and cook 15 minutes, uncovered, on medium heat. Return mixture to a boil on high heat and add shrimp. Cook 3 to 5 minutes, or until shrimp turn orange and are just done. Drain and serve shrimp on a table covered with newspaper or in bowls.
Serves 4.

From *Old Fashioned Country Favorites*
Published by Doubleday

Old Fashioned Vanilla Ice Cream with Homemade Chocolate Sauce

2 cups light cream	2 tablespoons dark brown sugar, packed
2½ cups heavy cream	
¾ cup superfine sugar	¼ cup chopped toasted natural almonds
1 teaspoon vanilla extract	
3 ounces semisweet chocolate, chopped	

For ice cream, combine light cream, 2 cups heavy cream, superfine sugar, and vanilla until sugar is dissolved. Transfer to an ice cream freezer, and freeze according to manufacturer's directions. Makes about 1½ quarts.

For sauce, melt chocolate over low heat in a saucepan. Stir in brown sugar and remaining cream, and cook 1 to 2 minutes, or until creamy.
Makes about ¾ cup.
Serve sauce over ice cream and top with toasted almonds.

From *Old Fashioned Country Favorites*
Published by Doubleday

Strawberry Shortcake

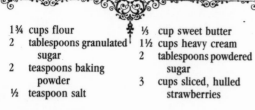

1¾ cups flour	⅓ cup sweet butter
2 tablespoons granulated sugar	1½ cups heavy cream
2 teaspoons baking powder	2 tablespoons powdered sugar
½ teaspoon salt	3 cups sliced, hulled strawberries

Preheat oven to 450°. In a bowl combine all dry ingredients except powdered sugar. Cut in butter until mixture resembles cornmeal. Stir in ⅔ cup cream until a dough forms. Roll out dough on a floured surface to ½" thickness. Cut out 6 rounds with a 3" biscuit cutter. Bake on a lightly buttered baking sheet 8 to 10 minutes, or until golden. Cool on a rack. Meanwhile, whip remaining cream with 1 tablespoon powdered sugar. Split cooled shortcakes in half. Cover bottom halves with strawberries and cream, and replace tops. Dust with remaining powdered sugar.
Makes 6.

From *Old Fashioned Country Favorites*
Published by Doubleday

Double Crust Apple Pie

Two 9-inch unbaked home-made pie shells, or frozen, thawed

4 medium Macoun, Winesap, McIntosh, or Granny Smith apples, unpeeled and thinly sliced

2 tablespoons lemon juice

¼ cup light brown sugar, packed

¼ cup golden raisins

1 teaspoon grated fresh ginger

1 teaspoon ground cinnamon

2 tablespoons sweet butter

1 egg yolk beaten with 1 tablespoon milk

Preheat oven to 425°. Fit one pie shell into a 9-inch baking pan. Place apples in a bowl and add lemon juice, sugar, raisins, ginger, and cinnamon, and toss to combine. Mound filling into crust and dot with butter. Top with second crust, pinching together dough to seal edges. Scallop edges by pressing with back of a teaspoon. Carefully cut a cross 4″ to 5″ long in each direction in center of crust. Peel back each section from center, as shown in photo. Lightly brush pastry with egg yolk mixture. Place in oven and bake 25 to 30 minutes, or until golden brown. Makes 1 pie.

From *Old Fashioned Country Favorites*
Published by Doubleday